Comprehensive Guide to Search Engine Optimization: From Beginner to Expert

Table of Contents

Chapter 1: Getting Started with SEO

Search Engine Optimization (SEO) is a critical process that ensures your website's content, regardless of your industry or target audience, meets the high standards set by search engines to earn a top-ranking position. When you implement SEO, you significantly increase the likelihood of your website appearing among the top search results. This is vital because most internet users tend to click on the first few search results they see when using search engines like Google. As your visibility improves and your website secures a top spot in search results, you gain the opportunity to convert these visitors into paying customers.

This is of utmost importance for both individuals and businesses because the majority of online searches commence with a search engine. In this book, we will explore all the essential aspects you need to succeed in the world of SEO and attract and retain loyal paying customers. Let's dive in.

In our digitally-dominated world, with social media and online activities playing significant roles, it has become imperative for businesses to establish a strong online presence. Companies are increasingly investing in professionals whose primary responsibility is to devise effective strategies for boosting their online traffic. This traffic, more often than not, flows in from search engines like Google. To cater to these search engines, SEO has evolved into an integral part of business operations.

Organic traffic generation is the preferred method for many, and for good reason. If you're tech-savvy and can keep up with the ever-evolving search engine algorithms, you can help ensure that your website remains prominently visible to these search engines. Strategies that focus on organic traffic generation are preferred across various website types because they naturally attract more customers to the products or services a business offers. In contrast, paid advertising, while effective in its own right, doesn't consistently yield the same high conversion rates as organic traffic generation in the long run. Additionally, paid advertising is often explicitly marked as such on the internet, which can discourage users from clicking on these ads. This means that converting users through paid advertising can be more challenging.

One highly effective approach to increase inbound traffic to any website is through SEO. Research has indicated that SEO can increase your website's traffic by a factor of 20 when compared to paid advertising, regardless of whether you're looking at desktop or mobile numbers.

SEO is not just about strategy; it's a marketing approach that continues to yield benefits over time. The key is to stay updated with the ever-evolving rules and guidelines set by major players in the search engine community. This includes paying close attention to incorporating the right keywords for all your content. These keywords help search engines rank your page more favorably. This ranking determines the order in which search results are displayed for user queries, ultimately giving your website the visibility you desire.

By crafting engaging and relevant content and incorporating the right keywords, you'll witness a significant boost in your traffic over time. In comparison, paid advertising requires continuous funding and doesn't always guarantee the desired results. However, SEO isn't just about strategic planning. It originally began as a way to inform search engines about your content and how it should be categorized. It was a method for search engines like Google to organize your content when users sought similar information. While this concept remains valid in theory, numerous advancements have occurred in the field of SEO, and we'll explore these developments in detail throughout this book.

But before we delve deeper, a common question that arises, especially for small and medium-sized businesses, is whether they should hire a specialist to handle SEO. The decision largely hinges on the time and effort you're willing to invest and the complexity of your website. For less intricate websites, you can start by implementing basic SEO strategies yourself. However, if you have plans for expansion, seeking guidance from an expert or hiring an agency may be beneficial. I'll provide further insights into this decision-making process later in this book.

Among the fundamental concepts you need to grasp are the mechanics of how SEO functions. This involves understanding the parameters used by leading search engines like Google and Bing to evaluate your website. Every search engine employs web crawlers to collect data about online content. These crawlers retrieve binary data (consisting of 0s and 1s), which is then used to create an index. This index undergoes an algorithmic assessment by the search engine to determine whether your website aligns with user queries. When you optimize your website for a search engine, you're ensuring that your content contains all the necessary information and metadata that users are likely to enter into the search bar. This metadata encompasses the correct title, description, and tags relevant to your content. It must be both pertinent and informative. Let's delve further into these concepts.

Chapter 2: Understanding the Basics of SEO

SEO, as previously mentioned, stands for "search engine optimization." When you practice SEO, you ensure that the quality and quantity of content on your website are geared towards increasing website traffic. This aims to enhance visibility and expose your brand to as many potential customers as possible. It's an organic approach to achieving better results when someone searches for information you may provide. SEO plays a pivotal role in promoting your product or service on the internet, given the trillions of online searches conducted each year and the countless websites vying for the same audience's attention.

Many of these websites are commercial entities, and search queries are a major avenue through which users discover brands and their offerings. When you execute effective search engine optimization, your website secures higher rankings for keywords and key phrases in search engine results. This boost in visibility offers a genuine opportunity to convert a casual website visitor into a paying customer. However, the once well-kept secret of SEO has become widely known, and businesses have become adept at optimizing their web pages to secure higher rankings and visibility.

Consequently, search engines continually refine their algorithms and ranking parameters, prioritizing user satisfaction over benefiting businesses with subpar content. Staying informed about these evolving practices is essential. Additionally, search engines aim to retain users on their search results pages (SERPs) rather than redirecting them to other websites because advertising is their primary revenue source. This explains the presence of specific features on the SERP.

Consider this: SERPs include both advertisements and organic results. One prominent feature is the "featured snippet" or "answer box," while image carousels serve a similar purpose but focus on images. These features offer users direct answers to specific questions, eliminating the need to visit another webpage. For instance, if a user types "London weather," "convert cm to inches," or "current time in Sydney," they receive a concise response within a designated box, rather than being directed to a website. This approach aims to enhance user experience by providing instant, relevant information. Search engines benefit from retaining users on the SERP for a brief period because they can serve more efficient advertisements.

Fortunately for businesses, effective search engine optimization techniques can ethically counteract some of these strategies. This applies to both paid and organic content. When a user enters a direct question into the search bar, a brief text summary from the highest-ranking page, which potentially answers the question directly, is displayed. This can be an organic result achieved through effective SEO.

Outsmarting strategies that aim to keep users on the SERP and redirecting them to your website requires strategic planning. This is why search engine optimization is a significant component of marketing strategies employed by companies, regardless of their size. At its core, SEO is about comprehending the words potential customers use when searching for your website and leveraging that knowledge to attract them to your site rather than your competitors'. Essentially, it's about understanding your customers. The good news is that the insights and techniques acquired through SEO are not confined to your website. They teach you how to use language effectively, a skill that can also enhance your website's visibility on social media platforms, which are magnets for online traffic.

The other aspect of this practice involves understanding what the crawlers employed by search engines seek to index and provide visibility. Search engines examine documents, images, videos, and various content types on your website. All this data is cataloged, a process known as "crawling" and "indexing," which represent two distinct phases. When a user enters a query, the indexed information is used to assess the relevance of your website's content to their query, determining your page's position in search results. Now, the first concept to grasp when discussing rankings is the critical role of keywords. That's the next topic we'll delve into.

Chapter 3: Exploring the World of Keyword Research

Keyword research is at the heart of effective search engine optimization (SEO). When we talk about keyword research, we're referring to the words and phrases that should be strategically incorporated into your website's content. Why? Because this strategic integration makes it effortless for users searching for specific information to discover your website when they enter particular words into the search bar. The goal is to align your understanding of user preferences with the data used by search engines, ensuring that your website ranks prominently when users search for those keywords. It's undeniably one of the most crucial aspects of SEO, giving you a competitive edge on the search engine results page (SERP). Moreover, it plays a pivotal role in your marketing efforts.

Starting the keyword research process typically involves creating a list of keywords relevant to the content you aim to optimize. It's a process that demands time and effort but yields exceptional results, making it a worthwhile investment of your resources. However, there's no one-size-fits-all approach to keyword research. It involves some trial and error, and it's not entirely arbitrary. For instance, there are certain things you should avoid. One common mistake is conducting keyword research only once and neglecting to update it periodically. Another misstep is solely focusing on the most popular keywords, resulting in your website competing with countless others using the same set of keywords.

Updating keywords is an ongoing necessity because the internet evolves continually. Staying current and adapting to changes is essential, as the language and preferences of your audience change. Whether you're managing a new website or maintaining an existing one, ensure that your content structure remains contemporary to resonate with potential visitors. This entails making sure your title and accompanying description reflect the content accurately. This humanizes your website, making it appear approachable and in touch with the present digital landscape.

Additionally, this approach keeps your webpage at the top of search results because these are the keywords users enter in the search bar. Therefore, the key takeaway is that keyword research is a continual process, requiring periodic refinement by eliminating outdated phrases and adding newer ones. It's crucial to strike a balance between competitive keywords and specific ones, ensuring you don't overlook niche audiences.

Diversifying your keyword list is equally vital. This entails using more than just the most popular keywords. Including some unique or less common keywords can give you an advantage in beating the competition. Numerous online tools are available to help you discover keywords related to your subject, but conducting your research and monitoring the outcomes of your trial-and-error methods are also essential. In the midst of these efforts, never compromise on the quality of your content. Regardless of how many keywords you include, if you can't engage and retain your visitors, no number of keywords will rescue your website.

Keyword research revolves around understanding the words and phrases that internet users enter into search bars, as well as assessing the popularity of these search terms. This knowledge also allows teams to explore how users research specific topics. By aligning your content with these words, you can create content that directly addresses users' questions, capitalizing on trending topics. In the industry, this practice is known as creating targeted content, and those who discover this content are more likely to spend time on your website, potentially recommending your products and services to others. They are also more likely to become paying customers.

Keyword research is invaluable to marketers for understanding buyer psychology, identifying high-demand keywords, and optimizing content. It not only informs you about popular keywords but also helps you beat the competition organically. It also provides insights into the language used by the demographic most likely to seek out your products or services.

However, finding keywords is only the beginning. To achieve the best results in terms of SEO, you must also know how to use keywords effectively. Start by identifying high-attention or long-tail keywords for your content and, if possible, incorporate them into the title and body of the text. Additionally, consider placing them in metadata elements like image file names and URLs. Be cautious not to overdo it—keyword density should be proportional to the amount of content on your website. Excessive keyword usage, known as keyword stuffing, is discouraged by search engines. Relevance consistently outweighs quantity.

Understanding keyword grouping is vital. This technique involves using a small set of relevant keywords for specific pages. For example, if you run an online automotive magazine, you'd gather all car-related keywords for that segment and break them down into sub-sections based on automobile brands. This approach ensures that all your pages are fundamentally optimized to some extent. Implementing this strategy involves:

Adding keywords to the URL
Incorporating keywords into the webpage's title
Using keyword variations in the body of the text
Including keywords in the description and meta tags
Utilizing keywords for image file names and alt text
Now, let's delve into a more advanced method of optimizing your website—on-page SEO, which we'll explore in the next chapter.

Chapter 4: Mastering On-Page SEO

Following the thorough examination of keyword research and optimization, the subsequent pivotal step is on-page optimization. This practice aims to fine-tune the technical aspects of your website, furthering your chances of securing a higher search engine ranking and, consequently, improving website traffic and conversion rates. Be aware, however, that the results of these efforts may not manifest immediately, so patience is a virtue in this endeavor.

On-page optimization involves a comprehensive review of both textual and visual elements, considering not only content but also the technical underpinnings in the website's HTML code and the user experience presented on the front end. Although there is also off-page optimization, which involves activities beyond your website such as external links and social media platforms, our focus for now will remain on the on-page factors.

This chapter represents a crucial aspect of search engine optimization that comes after meticulous keyword research. It empowers you to fine-tune the technical components of your web pages, increasing your prospects for higher search engine rankings. Now, don't be alarmed by the jargon; I'll simplify it for you to illustrate that it involves only a few adjustments.

4.1 Crafting Engaging Content

Content, as you know, is within your control. Just like the content, the technical details are also manageable by you, not solely the domain of programmers. On-page SEO optimization begins with content. A web page becomes valuable to a visitor only when the content proves useful. This is the foremost and primary criterion for users. Search engines share this perspective since users are their foremost concern. A search engine must provide relevant information to the user to be considered useful. Therefore, content plays a pivotal role in securing better rankings.

Effective SEO-oriented content is characterized by its ability to meet users' demands while also featuring a considerable number of resourceful and authoritative links, which are links pointing to the source of the information. Think of this as the principles of supply and demand in global markets. By satisfying the high demand for specific information, whether in the form of text, images, video, or audio, you create valuable content. Furthermore, when this content is easily linkable, it encourages others to link to it from their own content, thus driving traffic to your website. Why does this happen? Simply put, no one links to a page with subpar content, as it would only disappoint their own visitors. When your web page is linked within the content of other pages, it's akin to receiving a vote of confidence. This action elevates your web page's standing in the eyes of search engines.

4.2 Unveiling the Power of Title Tag

The title tag constitutes the second crucial on-page optimization element. Although we're delving into the realm of coding (particularly if you're utilizing an old-school website editor), don't worry. Most modern website builders feature user-friendly interfaces that simplify title tag editing for each of your pages.

The title tag is an HTML tag residing in the header section of every webpage. It serves as the initial context for your web page, visible in both the browser window and the search engine results page (SERP). Although it's not the sole determinant for organic ranking with a search engine, mishandling it with a poor title tag or duplicate versions can negate the progress achieved through other factors.

4.3 Navigating the World of URL

Beyond internal linking, on-page SEO also considers the structure of categories on your website. Let's illustrate this with an example. If your URL follows a logical order like "https://www.websitename.com/USnews/washington...," it's commendable as it transitions from general US news to the specifics of Washington. Search engines leverage this information to gauge a webpage's relevance.
This hierarchy aids search engines in indexing pages and categorizing them, particularly for users searching for localized Washington news. It's noteworthy that this process occurs before content evaluation.

Thus, URL hierarchy holds significant importance. In contrast, if your URL appears random like "https://www.websitename/report/washington17254...," it lacks hierarchy and fails to convey its purpose to search engines. Users typically don't search for terms like "report" and "washington17254." Consequently, such URLs hold no meaning for search engines, representing a missed opportunity.

4.4 Crafting Compelling Meta Description

The meta description, which has been pivotal in SEO since its inception, serves as the text beneath your page's title on the SERP. It provides users with a glimpse into your page's content and holds great importance. While its impact on Google rankings may have diminished compared to a decade ago, there is still evidence suggesting its significance. Consider it from the perspective of a user seeking quick information without navigating multiple pages. In such cases, meta descriptions prove invaluable, improving factors like the perceived quality of your webpage and the click-through rate (CTR).

4.5 Harnessing the Impact of Headlines

Headlines represent another critical facet of search engine optimization. Crafting compelling headlines for your blog posts may seem straightforward, yet it's surprising how many websites overlook keyword research for this aspect. A captivating headline not only captures user interest but also helps your content stand out on the SERP. Familiarity with the concept of clickbait highlights the importance of this aspect. However, resorting to clickbait strategies can have detrimental long-term consequences, as it erodes trust among visitors.

4.6 Enhancing User Experience

Lastly, user experience on the front end is a paramount concern. Most users lack technical expertise and prefer a seamless experience that facilitates easy access to desired information. Understand that new website visitors, those who have not previously explored your site, tend to be skeptical. Internet users are known for their impatience, emphasizing the need for a user-friendly website.

This necessitates a straightforward layout, pleasing color schemes, and an appealing overall design. Accomplishing these aspects sets a solid foundation for your site's usability.

In summary, on-page optimization entails a range of techniques to enhance your website's search engine visibility and user experience. By focusing on content, title tags, URLs, meta descriptions, headlines, and overall user experience, you can take significant strides in improving your website's performance and ranking.

Chapter 5: Building Strong and Relevant Backlinks

When you think about optimizing your website's content for search engines, one name stands out unmistakably: Google. And rightfully so. This tech giant places significant importance on links when ranking websites, more so than other search engines like Bing and Yahoo. Links serve as a crucial yardstick for search engines to discover more content and evaluate the quality of a web page. As mentioned earlier, when a website's link is embedded within the content of other websites, it's akin to receiving a positive review from the perspective of the search engine. It's like these websites are vouching for your content enough to redirect some of their traffic to your site. Therefore, every website must strive to construct a strong link profile. However, as time went on, some companies became a bit too cunning in this regard, overexploiting this aspect by inundating forums and comment sections on other websites with their links.

This prompted search engines to scrutinize more closely to detect unnatural patterns. Links of this nature are merely links for the sake of having them and don't genuinely benefit the users of any website. Nevertheless, link building remains an essential component, provided that the links align with the website users' interests. This can be achieved by ensuring that your links possess the following characteristics:

Usefulness to Website Visitors: The links should provide value to the visitors of a website.

Organic Placement: Links should be seamlessly integrated into the content and not appear forced.

Relevance and High-Quality Content: Links should direct users to pertinent and high-quality content.

Effective Anchor Text: The text used for linking (anchor text) should be well-crafted and relevant.

5.1 Distinguishing Good Links from Bad Links

Before delving into the various ways in which link building aids in SEO, let's differentiate between good and bad links from the perspective of search engines. Several factors come into play:

1. The Web Page's Authority: It's essential to secure links from authoritative websites. Search engines assess the quality of links based on the authority of the linking website. For instance, a backlink from Wall Street Journal or The New York Times carries far more weight than one from an obscure blogger.

2. Website Relevance: In addition to authority, the relevance of the linking website to your content matters. If you run a sports-oriented website, a link from an authoritative sports source is more valuable than one from an unrelated forum.

3. Link Placement on the Page: After considering authority and relevance, the position of the link within the content matters. A link placed high in the body of a page's text is more valuable than one relegated to the sidebar or footer.

4. Editorial Placement: The context in which the hyperlink's anchor text is placed is critical. If it's integrated naturally into the content and entices visitors to explore your content, it's considered editorially placed. Randomly placed links lacking context are not editorial in nature. Editorial links hold greater value for search engines than arbitrarily placed ones, which may even be viewed as unnatural and lead to penalties.

5. Anchor Text: The clickable part of a link, known as anchor text, is taken seriously by search engines, especially Google. If anchor text is overly keyword-stuffed, it may be deemed spammy.

5.2 Search Engines and Links

Search engines primarily use two types of links to assess website rankings: links that aid in discovering new content and links that contribute to ranking a web page. This determination occurs after web pages are crawled, and their content is indexed.

Once search engines are satisfied that the linking meets the criteria mentioned above and includes the right set of keywords, they're prepared to rank the page. This decision goes beyond evaluating page content; it also considers external links and the value of those linking websites. Accumulating high-value backlinks enhances your website's chances of ranking higher in search engine results.
However, excessive linking or over-optimization may lead to penalties by Google. Conversely, low-quality link building is a fruitless endeavor, as links from low-value websites won't

significantly impact your site's ranking. Striking a balance between the number of backlinks and their quality is essential. It's worth noting that high-quality backlinks are likely to drive substantial traffic to your website.

Building strong and relevant backlinks is essential for SEO success. By focusing on usefulness, organic placement, relevance, and anchor text, you can enhance your website's performance and search engine ranking.

Chapter 6: The Art of Executing an Effective Content Marketing Strategy

When discussing SEO for businesses, content marketing often doesn't receive the attention it deserves. Even some professionals overlook this aspect. However, after reading this chapter, you will have a better understanding. Alongside SEO, content marketing plays a pivotal role in modern marketing. When these two concepts are seamlessly combined and executed flawlessly, your website can become an unstoppable force. By devising a content marketing strategy with SEO in mind, your brand can maximize the benefits of any digital campaign. These strategies are commonly referred to as integrated strategies, as they bring together two potent concepts.

6.1 When SEO and Content Marketing Collide

In today's world, social media has become an integral part of both individuals' and businesses' lives. As customers frequent these platforms, businesses invest significant efforts in promoting their products and services on websites like Facebook, Twitter, Instagram, and more. Email marketing is another facet of internet marketing that yields promising results. However, these approaches don't guarantee reaching your desired demographic. Achieving that level of precision can be accomplished through integrated marketing strategies. For instance, when a customer has a question about a specific product or service, they promptly turn to a search engine and enter their query. Google and similar platforms then direct them to a website that can provide the answer.

When you aim to capture this segment of customers, optimizing your content provides a direct means of reaching them. It's all about offering them the right information at the right time. This is where search engine optimization and content marketing converge to benefit your brand.

6.2 The Process of Successful Execution

This process involves a few straightforward steps that, when implemented, allow you to reap substantial benefits. Here's how it works:

Step 1: Understand Your Audience
Optimizing your content revolves around making it easy for users to find the products or services they seek. Therefore, the

initial step is identifying who these customers are. Once you've accomplished that, you can create the type of content they're searching for. By optimizing it for SEO, you can tap into their queries and capture their attention. This can be achieved by asking and answering a few fundamental questions.

Begin by pinpointing your current customer base. Discovering who they are will lead you to data about their preferences and what more they expect from your brand. This data encompasses both qualitative and quantitative aspects. Therefore, conduct research on factors such as age, gender, purchase history, and engagement with your website or brand. This will provide you with a rough profile of your average existing customer. The next data point involves identifying your competition. Observe what your demographic is seeking from your competitors and why they are choosing those brands. This information is often readily available on social media profiles, customer reviews, and comments on authoritative blogs. When you come across customers who are satisfied with your competition, you'll gain insights into areas where you might be lacking. Similarly, when you find customers who are dissatisfied with the competition, you'll ascertain whether that's a space you can fill. This process leads you to determine what you can offer to entice your competition's customers to switch to your brand. This necessitates considering the products or services you currently provide and the demographic that benefits from them. Combine this with the information you've gathered about your competition, and you can identify gaps. Lastly, understand your brand's value in the current market. Find out what your existing and potential customers think about your services and products. Additionally, uncover areas where you excel and areas that require improvement. You can gather this information through simple surveys on social media or your own website. The answers to these questions will help you segment your customer base and construct your buyer persona. With this knowledge, you can create content tailored to this demographic. When you optimize it for search engines, you can reach them more effectively and drive traffic to your website. When the content is of high quality, you'll have the potential to convert them into paying customers or strengthen loyalty among existing customers.

Step 2: Define Your Brand
Now that you understand your audience and what they seek, along with insights into your competition and what they offer, you have the opportunity to define or redefine your brand. Identify current topics of discussion and create content accordingly. Ensure that you establish your voice as an authority on the subject. If this requires additional work and research, invest resources in it because, in the long run, you'll witness significant results. Your content must be unique and not simply a rehash of existing material. Strive to stand out, not just with language but also with insights.

Step 3: Conduct Keyword Research
Conduct comprehensive keyword research to gain a deep understanding of this crucial aspect.

Step 4: Create Exceptional Content
Once you've identified unique content topics and relevant keywords to reach your target audience, take your content beyond blogs. Consider expanding your website to include long-form content such as white papers and ebooks. Videos are a substantial part of the SEO landscape, so consider allocating resources in that direction if you haven't already. If you want your customers to stay on your page and explore your offerings further, you need to go beyond keywords. This is where the research you conducted to create unique content topics becomes invaluable. Craft high-quality content that resonates with both customers and search engines. This approach also helps you avoid search engine penalties for low-quality content. To enhance your content beyond the obvious, consider these points:

Ensure your blog posts are well-written and free of spelling or grammatical errors, as these issues can detract from your brand's credibility. Structure your pieces effectively to ensure a seamless flow from one idea to the next.
Incorporate examples to simplify the understanding of your concepts. Avoid using technical language that the average reader may not comprehend. If you must use such terminology, provide brief definitions or include a glossary, especially in ebooks. This approach fosters a stronger connection between customers and your brand.

Given your understanding of your audience's demographic, use their language. Be friendly and conversational in tone to prevent readers from feeling like they're digesting information generated by a machine.

Pay attention to formatting. Utilize bullet points and concise paragraphs to prevent reader fatigue. Periodically summarize key points for those quickly scanning the page.

Step 5: Keep Your Content Updated

The final step involves staying ahead in the content game. This can be achieved by updating content that remains relevant long after its initial publication. You're aware of the benefits of updating headlines, descriptions, keywords, and tags. Explore the possibility of adding information to make the content pertinent to the present day. In addition to these strategies, consider the following:

Integrate fun facts or statistics to maintain relevance.

Optimize metadata for your preferred search engine.

Regularly review your website traffic statistics and assess your content.

In essence, when a blog post continues to perform well weeks or months after its publication, seize the opportunity to capitalize on the traffic it receives by updating it and aligning it with any relevant trends.

In conclusion, the fusion of SEO and content marketing can empower your brand to achieve remarkable success in the digital landscape when executed diligently and strategically.

Chapter 7: Unveiling 10 SEO Best Practices

When discussing the best practices for SEO, you'll often come across the terms "white hat SEO" and "black hat SEO." Don't let the jargon intimidate you; these are simple and opposing concepts. White hat techniques are those that enhance your website's reputation with search engines through ethical practices aimed at providing users with high-quality content. This, in turn, leads to better search engine rankings. On the other hand, black hat techniques are the opposite – they involve using cheap tricks to deceive search engines, resulting in ethical concerns and the risk of penalties.

Thankfully, these definitions aren't arbitrary, and the penalties associated with black hat SEO should be taken seriously due to their real-time business consequences. While shortcuts may seem tempting in the short term, the risks are too high, and they are often not worth pursuing. Some black hat techniques include link scraping and keyword stuffing, which can not only lead to heavy penalties but also result in your website being removed from search results, a practice known as "blacklisting."

7.1 Strategic Keyword Placement

One of the fundamental aspects of successful search engine optimization is strategic keyword placement. When you have a set of valuable keywords, it's natural to want to use them to enhance your content's visibility. However, it's crucial to exercise caution and strategy.

Strategic keyword placement goes beyond merely inserting keywords into your content. It involves a deep understanding of how these keywords are relevant to your content. So, what exactly does "strategic keyword placement" entail?

Strategic keyword placement entails not only inserting keywords into the text but also having a comprehensive grasp of how these keywords are relevant to your content. Here are some key considerations:

Primary Keyword: Identify the primary keyword that best represents your content's theme. This primary keyword should appear early in your content, ideally within the opening paragraphs.

Natural Usage: Avoid overusing keywords, a practice known as "keyword stuffing." Keywords should be seamlessly integrated into the context of your content, ensuring that the text remains clear and readable to users.

Keyword Variations: Consider keyword variations and related phrases. This helps cover a broader range of searches and attracts a more diverse audience.

Relevance: Ensure that keywords are highly relevant to your content. Google also assesses the alignment between keywords and the topic discussed in your content.

Monitoring and Optimization: Continuously monitor the performance of your keywords over time and make necessary optimizations. Keywords that perform well can be retained, while underperforming ones can be reevaluated.

In essence, strategic keyword placement goes beyond the physical positioning of keywords in the text; it also involves their relevance and thoughtful usage. This approach will enhance the visibility of your content on search engines, attracting a broader and more engaged audience.

7.2 Deciphering Search Intent

Deciphering user search intent is a critical aspect of effective search engine optimization. Google places a high priority on understanding why users are conducting specific searches because it allows the search engine to deliver more relevant results. Search intent can be categorized into four primary types, each with its unique characteristics:

Informational Intent: This type of search is characterized by users seeking direct answers to specific queries. For example, a user searching for "how to change a flat tire" is seeking step-by-step instructions on this task. Recognizing informational intent requires crafting content that provides clear and informative responses to common queries within your niche.

Navigational Intent: Navigational searches are conducted when users are looking for a particular website or web page. For instance, someone searching for "Facebook login" is seeking quick access to the Facebook platform. Optimizing for navigational intent involves ensuring that your website is easily accessible to users searching for your brand or platform.

Transactional Intent: Users with transactional intent are on the verge of making a purchase. They are actively looking for a product, service, or tool to facilitate a transaction. For example, a search for "buy iPhone 13" indicates a strong intent to make a purchase. To cater to transactional intent, it's essential to provide clear product descriptions, pricing, and purchase options on your e-commerce site.

Commercial Investigation Intent: This type of search involves users who are researching products or services before making a decision. They often seek "best of" lists or comparisons within specific product categories. For instance, someone searching for "best digital cameras 2023" is likely comparing options before buying. To address commercial investigation intent, consider creating comprehensive guides, reviews, or comparison content that assists users in making informed choices.

By recognizing these distinct search intents, you can tailor your content to align with what users are actively seeking. This approach not only enhances your search engine rankings but also ensures that your content resonates with your target audience, driving higher engagement and conversions.

7.3 Accelerating Page Loading Speed

One of the pivotal elements in modern SEO best practices is ensuring that your web pages load swiftly. Page loading speed is not solely a matter of user convenience; it's also a critical aspect of search engine optimization. Let's delve deeper into why it holds such paramount importance and how you can enhance it.

User Experience and Bounce Rates: First and foremost, consider the user experience. When visitors land on your website, they expect it to load quickly and efficiently. In an era of instant gratification, people are increasingly impatient when it comes to waiting for web pages to load. If your site is sluggish, users are more likely to abandon it in favor of faster alternatives. High bounce rates signal to search engines that your content may not be as relevant or valuable, potentially affecting your rankings.

Conversion Rates: Page loading speed also has a direct impact on your conversion rates. Research has shown that even a mere one-second delay in page loading can result in a seven percent reduction in conversion rates. This means that a slower website translates into fewer leads, sales, or other desired actions. To maximize your website's effectiveness, you must prioritize fast-loading pages.

Search Engine Favor: Search engines, particularly Google, take page speed seriously when ranking websites. They understand that slow-loading pages frustrate users, leading to a poor overall experience. Consequently, search engines are more inclined to rank faster-loading pages higher in search results. By optimizing your page loading speed, you increase your chances of ranking well and attracting organic traffic.

Mobile Responsiveness: With the increasing prevalence of mobile device usage for web browsing, page speed on mobile platforms has become even more critical. Google, in particular, prioritizes mobile-first indexing, which means it primarily uses the mobile version of the content for ranking and indexing. Ensuring your web pages load swiftly on mobile devices is imperative for maintaining and improving your search engine rankings.

Optimization Techniques: To accelerate your page loading speed, consider implementing several optimization techniques:

- **Minimize Plugins**: As mentioned earlier, one effective strategy is to reduce or eliminate non-essential plugins. Each plugin adds code and functionality that can slow down your website. Evaluate which plugins are truly necessary for your site's functionality and remove the rest.

- **Compress Images**: Large image files are often a primary culprit for slow-loading pages. Compressing images without compromising quality can significantly reduce loading times. Utilize image compression tools or plugins to automate this process.

- **Browser Caching**: Implement browser caching to store certain elements of your website on a visitor's device. This allows returning visitors to experience faster load times as their browser retrieves cached data instead of re-downloading it.

- **Content Delivery Networks (CDNs)**: CDNs distribute your website's content across multiple servers located in various geographic regions. This reduces the physical distance data must travel, resulting in faster loading times for users worldwide.

- **Code Optimization**: Streamline your website's code by removing unnecessary characters, spaces, and line breaks. This minimizes file sizes and improves load times.

By taking these steps to enhance your page loading speed, you'll not only provide a better user experience but also improve your website's search engine rankings and overall performance. In the competitive landscape of the internet, speed can make all the difference.

7.4 Securing Your Website with HTTPS

One of the critical aspects of modern SEO best practices is ensuring the security of your website by implementing HTTPS. Let's delve deeper into why HTTPS is crucial, its impact on SEO rankings, and how to secure your website with it.

Enhanced Security: HTTPS, which stands for HyperText Transfer Protocol Secure, provides an added layer of security to your website. It achieves this by encrypting the data exchanged between your web server and users' devices. This encryption makes it extremely difficult for malicious actors to intercept and decipher any sensitive information transmitted, such as login credentials, personal data, or payment details.

Trust and Credibility: Websites that use HTTPS display a padlock icon or a "Secure" label in the browser's URL bar. This visual indicator signals to visitors that your site is secure and that their data is protected during their interaction with your site. This, in turn, enhances the trustworthiness and credibility of your website, instilling confidence in your audience.

SEO Rankings: Google has been prioritizing website security and user privacy for several years.

In 2014, Google officially announced that HTTPS would be considered a ranking factor in its search algorithm. This means that websites using HTTPS receive a slight ranking boost compared to their non-secure counterparts. While it may not be the most influential ranking factor, it still contributes to your site's overall SEO performance.

Data Privacy and Compliance: With the increasing focus on data privacy regulations like the General Data Protection Regulation (GDPR) and the California Consumer Privacy Act (CCPA), securing user data is not just good practice; it's often a legal requirement. Using HTTPS helps you comply with these regulations by safeguarding user data.

How to Implement HTTPS: Securing your website with HTTPS involves several steps:

Obtain an SSL Certificate: The first step is to obtain an SSL (Secure Sockets Layer) certificate. You can acquire one from your web hosting provider or through a trusted SSL certificate authority. Some web hosts offer free SSL certificates, while others may charge for them.

Install the SSL Certificate: Once you have the SSL certificate, you'll need to install it on your web server. This process varies depending on your hosting provider and server configuration. Many hosting companies offer step-by-step guides or even automated tools to assist with the installation.

Update Your Website Links: After installing the SSL certificate, ensure that all internal and external links on your website use the "https://" protocol instead of "http://." This ensures that users are always directed to the secure version of your site.

Update Search Engines: It's a good practice to inform search engines about the change to HTTPS. You can do this by updating your sitemap and submitting it through Google Search Console or other search engine webmaster tools.

Monitor and Test: Regularly monitor your website to ensure that the SSL certificate is active and functioning correctly. Perform periodic security tests to identify and address any vulnerabilities.

By following these steps and implementing HTTPS on your website, you not only enhance security but also contribute to improved SEO rankings, user trust, and compliance with data privacy regulations. It's a crucial aspect of modern web development and SEO that should not be overlooked.

Addressing Duplicate Content Challenges

One of the critical aspects of achieving success in search engine optimization (SEO) is effectively addressing challenges related to duplicate content. Google strictly prohibits the presence of duplicate or near-duplicate content on different pages of your website. This includes not only visible text but also elements like title tags, product pages, landing pages, meta descriptions, alt text for images, and more. In this section, we will delve deeper into the importance of tackling the issue of duplicate content and how to do so effectively.

Why Duplicate Content Is a Problem: Google considers duplicate content as a hindrance to user experience and search result diversity. When different pages on your site contain the same or similar content, Google may struggle to determine which page to show users in search results. This could lead to lower rankings in search engine results pages (SERPs) or even penalties.

7.5 Tackling Duplicate Content Challenges

Identify Duplicate Content: The first step is to identify areas on your website where there might be duplicate or similar content. This may require a thorough analysis of your web pages, including titles, descriptions, page text, and more.

Review and Update: Once duplicate content is identified, carefully review each instance. Consider whether changes can be made to make the content unique. This could involve rewriting text, adding additional information, or modifying titles.

Consider Consolidation: If you have many similar pages with nearly identical content, you may want to consider consolidation. Merge similar content into a single high-quality page. Ensure you redirect old URLs to the new ones to avoid 404 errors.

Utilize the Canonical Tag: The canonical tag is an HTML label that allows webmasters to indicate the preferred version of a page when there are different similar variants. By using the canonical tag, you can tell Google which page should be considered the original or primary one.

Use Webmaster Tools: Webmaster tools like Google Search Console provide reports on duplicate content. Use these tools to identify and address duplicate content issues.

Avoid Manipulative Purposes: Some webmasters attempt to use duplicate content as a manipulative strategy to try to achieve higher rankings. These practices are generally detected and penalized by search engines. Avoid such practices.

Follow Google's Guidelines: For in-depth guidance on handling duplicate content, refer to Google's official guidelines. These guidelines provide valuable information on how Google treats duplicate content and how you can avoid issues.

Addressing challenges related to duplicate content is crucial to enhancing the overall quality of your website and optimizing search engine rankings. Make sure to pay attention to this aspect as part of your overall SEO strategy.

7.6 Enhancing Your Images for SEO

Images play a crucial role in enhancing the visual appeal and engagement of your website's content. However, it's important to note that unoptimized images can have a detrimental impact on your site's performance, particularly in terms of page loading times. In this section, we will explore the significance of optimizing your images for SEO and provide insights into best practices for doing so effectively.

Why Image Optimization Matters for SEO

Page Speed Improvement: Large, unoptimized images can significantly slow down the loading times of your web pages. Since page speed is a vital factor for both user experience and search engine rankings, optimizing images can lead to faster-loading pages and improved SEO.

User Experience: Users tend to have a shorter attention span when browsing websites. If your pages take too long to load due to unoptimized images, visitors are more likely to leave, resulting in higher bounce rates. Optimized images contribute to a smoother and more enjoyable user experience.

Mobile Responsiveness: With a growing number of users accessing websites via mobile devices, it's crucial to ensure that images are optimized for various screen sizes and resolutions. Mobile-friendly images contribute to better mobile responsiveness, which is a factor considered by search engines.

Best Practices for Image Optimization:

Choose the Right Format: Select the appropriate image format based on the type of image. JPEG is ideal for photographs and images with many colors, while PNG is suitable for images with transparency or simple graphics. WebP is a modern format known for its compression efficiency.

Resize Images: Resize images to their display dimensions on your website. Avoid uploading images that are larger than necessary, as this can lead to longer loading times.

Compress Images: Utilize image compression techniques to reduce file sizes while maintaining visual quality. Various online tools and plugins are available for this purpose.

Add Descriptive Alt Text: For each image, include descriptive alt text that provides context and relevance. Alt text serves not only as accessibility support but also contributes to SEO, as search engines rely on alt text to understand image content.

Use Image Sitemaps: Include images in your XML sitemap. This helps search engines discover and index your images, potentially leading to enhanced visibility in image search results.

Implement Lazy Loading: Lazy loading is a technique that defers the loading of off-screen images until the user scrolls to them. This can improve initial page load times and save bandwidth.

Responsive Images: Utilize responsive image techniques, such as the "srcset" attribute in HTML, to deliver appropriately sized images to different devices and screen resolutions.

Image File Names: Use descriptive and relevant file names for your images. Avoid generic file names like "image001.jpg" and instead opt for names that reflect the image's content.

By incorporating these best practices into your image optimization strategy, you can significantly enhance your website's SEO performance while providing a seamless and visually appealing experience for your visitors. Remember that image optimization is an integral part of overall SEO, and neglecting it can result in missed opportunities for improved rankings and user engagement.

7.7 Integrating Relevant Hyperlinks

Incorporating relevant hyperlinks within your content is a crucial practice for enhancing your SEO strategy. In this section, we will explore the importance of integrating relevant hyperlinks in your content and how this practice can contribute to improving user experience and the authority of your website.

Why Link Integration is Important for SEO:

Enhancing User Experience: Hyperlinks to relevant and informative pages provide your visitors with additional resources to delve into related topics. This enriches the user experience, allowing them to easily find further relevant information.

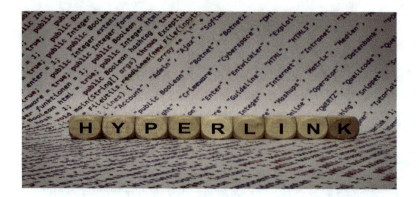

Providing Credibility and Authority: When you link to authoritative and reliable sources, you demonstrate your thorough research and industry knowledge. This helps build credibility for your website in the eyes of both visitors and search engines.

Potential Reciprocal Links: When you provide links to other sources, there's a chance that those sources may notice your site, and if they find value in your content, they may reciprocate by linking back to you. These reciprocal links can further enhance the authority of your website.

How to Integrate Relevant Hyperlinks:

Choose Reliable Sources: Ensure that you link only to trustworthy and authoritative sources. This includes websites of recognized companies, government entities, reputable organizations, and respected publications. Avoid linking to low-quality or spammy websites.

Relevance to Content: Links should be relevant to the surrounding content. Make sure that the anchor text (the link text) clearly reflects the topic the link pertains to.

New Window Opening (Optional): When linking to external content, you can choose whether to open the link in a new browser window or the same window. This depends on your preference and how you want to influence user behavior.

Descriptive Anchor Text: Use descriptive anchor text that clearly communicates the subject of the link. Avoid generic anchor text like "click here" or "read more."

Balance the Number of Links: Avoid inserting an excessive number of links within a single page, as this could be considered spammy. Maintain a natural balance and link only when relevant.

Monitor Links: Periodically, check the hyperlinks within your content to ensure they are still active and lead to the intended resources.

Integrating relevant hyperlinks is a key practice for improving the SEO of your website. Not only does it enhance user experience and the credibility of your site, but it can also open up opportunities for collaboration with other sources in your industry. Always remember to use this practice strategically and relevantly to maximize the benefits of SEO.

7.8 Leveraging the Insights from Keyword Research

In this section, we'll delve deeper into the critical practice of leveraging the insights gained from keyword research to enhance your website's visibility and SEO performance. Keyword research is a fundamental aspect of optimizing your online content, and understanding how to effectively utilize these insights can make a significant difference in your SEO strategy.

The Significance of Keyword Research:

Keyword research serves as the foundation for creating content that resonates with your target audience and ranks well in search engine results. Here's why it's crucial:

Understanding User Behavior: Keyword research helps you gain insights into how your potential customers search for information, products, or services online. This understanding is invaluable for tailoring your content to match user intent.

Enhancing Relevance: By identifying relevant keywords, you can align your content with the topics and phrases that matter most to your audience. This increases the chances of your content being seen by users genuinely interested in your offerings.

Competitive Analysis: Keyword research allows you to evaluate the keyword landscape within your industry. You can identify keywords that your competitors are targeting and discover gaps or opportunities to differentiate yourself.

Effective Strategies for Leveraging Keyword Research:

High-Volume Keywords: Identify high-volume keywords relevant to your industry and offerings. These keywords typically have a higher search volume, indicating a greater potential for traffic.

Long-Tail Keywords: Don't overlook long-tail keywords – longer, more specific keyword phrases. While they may have lower search volumes individually, they often have higher conversion rates because they align closely with user intent.

Keyword Placement: Integrate your chosen keywords naturally within your content, including in titles, headings, and throughout the body. Ensure that keyword usage feels organic and enhances the readability of your content.

Content Creation: Develop content that comprehensively addresses the topics related to your keywords. Offer valuable insights, solutions, or information to satisfy user intent thoroughly.

Diversify Keywords: Avoid over-reliance on a single keyword or keyword phrase. Diversify your keyword usage to cover a range of relevant terms. This broadens your content's reach.

Regular Updates: Periodically revisit your keyword research to stay up-to-date with evolving search trends and user behavior. Update your content accordingly to maintain its relevance.

Competitor Analysis: Analyze the keywords your competitors are targeting. Identify opportunities to rank for keywords they may have overlooked or areas where you can outperform them.

Tracking and Analytics: Implement tracking tools and analytics to monitor the performance of your chosen keywords. Measure their impact on your website's traffic, engagement, and conversions.

Leveraging the insights obtained from keyword research is not a one-time task but an ongoing practice. By continually optimizing your content with relevant and strategically chosen keywords, you can strengthen your website's visibility, attract a more qualified audience, and ultimately achieve better SEO results.

7.9 Maximizing Google Search Console

Google Search Console provides a wealth of valuable insights into your website's performance on search engine results pages. It offers comprehensive reports and tools to help you understand and improve various aspects of your website's search presence. Here are some key ways to maximize the benefits of Google Search Console:

Performance Analysis: Dive deep into the performance report to understand how your website is performing in Google Search. Analyze data on clicks, impressions, click-through rates, and average position. Identify which queries are driving traffic to your site and which pages are ranking well. Use this information to refine your content and SEO strategy.

Mobile Usability: With mobile devices accounting for a significant portion of web traffic, it's crucial to ensure that your website is mobile-friendly. Google Search Console provides insights into mobile usability issues on your site. Address any mobile usability errors to improve the user experience for mobile visitors.

Index Coverage: The index coverage report reveals how well Googlebot can crawl and index your site's pages. Check for any crawl errors, indexing issues, or pages that are excluded from search results. Fixing these issues can help ensure that your content is properly indexed and accessible to users.

Sitemap Submission: Submitting an XML sitemap of your website to Google Search Console can help search engines discover and crawl your pages more efficiently. Ensure that your sitemap is up to date and contains all relevant URLs.

URL Inspection: Use the URL inspection tool to check the indexing status of specific pages on your website. You can request indexing for new or updated pages, ensuring that they appear in search results faster.

Security Issues: Monitor the security issues section to be alerted to any potential security threats or issues affecting your site. Promptly address any security concerns to protect your website and users.

Performance Enhancements: Regularly review the Core Web Vitals report to assess your site's loading performance, interactivity, and visual stability. Google considers these factors when ranking websites, so optimizing your site's performance can lead to improved search rankings.

Structured Data: If you use structured data on your site to enhance search results with rich snippets, Google Search Console provides insights into any errors or enhancements related to structured data markup.

Manual Actions: Check for any manual actions taken by Google's webspam team against your site. If you receive a manual action, follow Google's guidelines for resolving the issue and requesting a reconsideration review.

Search Appearance: Explore the various search appearance options in Google Search Console, such as rich results, AMP, and job postings. Ensure that your site is eligible for these features and that they are correctly implemented.

By maximizing the use of Google Search Console, you can gain a deeper understanding of how your website performs in search results and take proactive steps to improve its visibility and user experience. Regularly monitor the provided insights and implement recommended optimizations to stay competitive in the online landscape.

7.10 Embracing Long-Form Content

Long-form content, often dismissed in favor of shorter pieces, still holds a strong position in the realm of SEO and content marketing.

Research consistently shows that longer articles, typically surpassing the 3,000-word mark, tend to outperform their shorter counterparts in various aspects. Here's why you should embrace long-form content as a valuable part of your content strategy:

1. **Enhanced Search Performance**: Long-form content has a higher likelihood of ranking well on search engine results pages (SERPs). Google and other search engines tend to favor comprehensive, in-depth content that thoroughly addresses user queries. By providing detailed information, you increase your chances of appearing at the top of search results.

2. **Increased Traffic**: Long-form articles tend to attract more organic traffic over time. They serve as comprehensive resources that users bookmark, share, and revisit. This sustained interest can result in a steady flow of visitors to your website, ultimately boosting your online presence.

3. **More Social Shares**: Research indicates that longer content pieces receive more shares on social media platforms. When your content offers valuable insights, solutions, or in-depth analysis, readers are more likely to share it with their networks, extending your reach and potentially attracting new audiences.

4. **Higher Backlink Potential**: Long-form content often attracts more backlinks from other websites. When you provide extensive and well-researched information, other content creators and websites are more inclined to reference and link to your content as a reputable source. This can significantly improve your website's authority in the eyes of search engines.

5. **Establishing Authority**: Long-form content allows you to establish yourself or your brand as an authority in your niche or industry. In-depth articles showcase your expertise, knowledge, and commitment to delivering valuable information. Over time, this can lead to increased trust among your audience.

6. **Comprehensive Coverage**: Longer content pieces provide the opportunity to comprehensively cover a topic. You can address various aspects, answer multiple questions, and offer diverse perspectives within a single article. This not only caters to a broader audience but also encourages readers to spend more time on your website.

7. **Improved User Experience**: While content length alone isn't the sole factor for a positive user experience, long-form content often includes visual elements, subheadings, and well-structured information. These elements enhance readability and engagement, contributing to an overall positive user experience.

8. **Diversified Content Portfolio**: Incorporating long-form content into your strategy diversifies your content portfolio. By offering a mix of short, medium, and long articles, you can cater to different audience preferences and search intents, expanding your potential reach.

When you decide to incorporate long-form content, it's crucial to emphasize quality, relevance, and user engagement. While longer articles have their strengths, they must genuinely benefit your audience. Conduct comprehensive research, structure your information logically, and include visual elements to craft compelling and informative long-form content that captivates both users and search engines.

In conclusion, adhering to these SEO best practices can lead to enhancements in your website's search engine rankings and its overall performance.

Chapter 8: Exploring Advanced SEO Tactics

In the ever-evolving landscape of digital marketing, it's essential not just to know the fundamentals of SEO but to also delve into advanced strategies that can give you a competitive edge. This chapter serves as your gateway to the world of advanced SEO tactics, offering insights and guidance to help you take your digital campaigns to the next level.

8.1 Creating Effective Topic Clusters

Imagine your content strategy as a constellation of interconnected ideas, all orbiting around a central theme, akin to celestial bodies gravitating towards a guiding star. This concept is known as "Topic Clusters," and it's a powerful method to structure your content for both users and search engines.

Here's how it works: you begin with a central, overarching topic that forms the nucleus of your content strategy. This central theme is supported by a constellation of related subtopics, each explored in-depth through separate content pieces. These subtopics are meticulously linked back to the main topic, creating a seamless network of interrelated content.

The advantages of employing topic clusters are multifaceted. Firstly, it keeps visitors engaged on your site for longer periods as they explore the various facets of a subject that interests them. This extended dwell time can have a positive impact on your search engine rankings. Secondly, it allows you to place hyperlinks strategically among related topics, optimizing your site's internal linking structure.

Think of topic clusters as a departure from traditional long-form content; instead, it's a dynamic, interconnected web of information that showcases your authority on a particular subject.

8.2 Conducting Comprehensive SEO Audits

One of the most potent ways to elevate your SEO game is by conducting a comprehensive SEO audit. This process entails a systematic evaluation of your website's performance, uncovering critical insights that can bridge the gap between sales and search traffic.

While you have the option to enlist the expertise of professionals for this task, understanding the fundamental principles behind an SEO audit can empower you to perform it independently. Think of an SEO audit as a diagnostic check-up for your website, designed to identify strengths, weaknesses, and opportunities for improvement.

Here's what an SEO audit typically involves:

Optimized Titles and Descriptions: Ensure that all your content features titles and descriptions optimized with relevant keywords to enhance search engine visibility.

Proper Keyword Integration: Strike the right balance with keywords, avoiding the pitfall of keyword stuffing, which can negatively impact your rankings.

Structured URLs: Simplify and structure your URLs effectively, conveying to search engines the content's topic and purpose.

Content Formatting: Organize your content with clear headings and subheadings, making it more reader-friendly. Each paragraph should comprise at least 2-3 sentences, and important points can be emphasized with bold or italics. Don't forget to incorporate a call to action whenever relevant.

Image Optimization: Images are integral to web content, but unoptimized images can hinder page loading times. Optimize images for size and load speed, and don't forget to add descriptive alt text to enhance accessibility and SEO.

Inclusion of Relevant Links: Strengthen your content by incorporating authoritative internal and external links. This not only enriches the user experience but also signals to search engines the credibility and relevance of your content.

8.3 Identifying Valuable Journalist Keywords

Journalists often rely on Google to source specific data and statistics that enrich their articles. By strategically targeting "journalist keywords," you can position your website as a valuable resource, increasing the likelihood of earning backlinks from their articles.

When you use keywords that align with what journalists are likely searching for, you provide your website with an excellent opportunity to be cited as a source in their articles. This not only results in valuable backlinks but also establishes a mutually beneficial relationship. Journalists appreciate having reliable sources for their work, and in return, your website gains both recognition and inbound traffic.

8.4 Strengthening Internal Link Structures

Internal linking is an often underestimated SEO technique that can have a significant impact on your website's search engine ranking. When you strategically link different pieces of content within your website, you send a clear signal to search engines that you offer valuable information across your domain.

Here's how it works: when one page on your website links to another, it creates a path for search engine crawlers to follow.

This allows them to discover and index new content more efficiently. By consistently implementing a robust internal linking strategy, you enhance your website's overall search engine visibility.

Additionally, the anchor text used in these internal links plays a crucial role. When anchor text is relevant and descriptive, it provides search engines with valuable context about the linked page's content, further improving your rankings.

8.5 Optimizing Dynamic Parameters

Efficient search engine crawling and indexing are essential for improving your website's search engine rankings. Employing dynamic parameters, such as pagination, is a strategic approach to achieving this.

Pagination involves dividing your content into multiple pages, a common practice on e-commerce websites to manage extensive product listings. To optimize this process, you'll want to reformat your URLs effectively. For instance, consider transforming a lengthy URL like this:

Before: https://yourwebsite.com/sports-topics/page/5

Into a more search-engine-friendly format:

After: https://yourwebsite.com/athletics-topics?page=5

This small adjustment helps Google recognize your paginated URLs as distinct and prevents the unnecessary re-crawling of identical pages. As a result, your content gets indexed more efficiently, bringing you one step closer to achieving higher search engine rankings.

Incorporating these advanced SEO tactics into your digital strategy can significantly enhance your online visibility and overall performance. As the digital landscape continues to evolve, staying at the forefront of SEO practices will ensure your sustained success in the competitive online realm.

Chapter 9: Measuring and Monitoring SEO Results

Whether you are using Google Analytics (which is recommended) or another service, it's crucial to keep track of how your SEO strategies are performing. This allows you to assess which tactics are effectively boosting your content and what steps need to be taken regarding strategies that aren't yielding the desired results. Do you need to make adjustments, or is it time to pivot entirely? The answers to these questions can be found through data analysis. While you can hire an SEO expert to provide insights, understanding the primary parameters that reveal the effectiveness of your strategies is not overly complicated. Let's provide you with an overview of the key metrics that offer insights into how your SEO efforts are unfolding so that you can interpret the data effectively.

9.1 Analyzing Organic Traffic

Understanding how well your website performs in terms of organic search traffic is paramount. This traffic comprises visitors who arrive at your site through search engine results pages, often in response to specific keywords or phrases they've entered into the search bar. It's crucial to delve into the details of this traffic source.

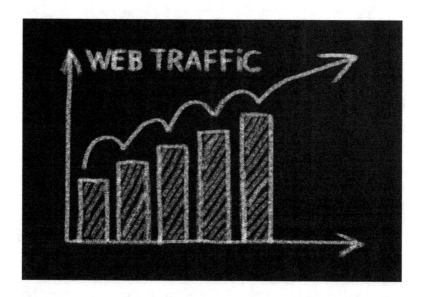

The number of visitors your site attracts through organic search is your first significant metric to assess. This metric is particularly valuable because it represents targeted traffic. These users are actively seeking specific information, and if your website provides the answers they seek, you're more likely to rank high in search results. This, in turn, increases the likelihood of converting these visitors into paying customers.

A strong performance in organic traffic also indicates the effectiveness of your overall organic SEO strategy. When your website enjoys high visibility in search results, it signifies that your efforts to optimize content, keywords, and other SEO elements are paying off.

By scrutinizing your organic traffic data, you can gain valuable insights into the health of your website's online presence and identify opportunities for improvement.

9.2 Evaluating the Quality of SEO Traffic

The best way to determine whether the traffic you are getting is quality traffic or not is to check the increase or decrease in the conversion rate. This means you need to inspect whether the people coming to your site are buying your product or service. If they are new users, are they getting converted into paid customers? There are several tools that can tell you if and when this is happening. You can even compare the numbers from this week or month to the previous one to see if it's getting better or worse. You can also learn about multiple visits and if those visits led to any purchases. If the overall traffic is consistent but the conversion rate goes down, you might not be getting high-quality traffic. Because it means that people are visiting the site but not buying your product or service. On the contrary, if you make a change and say start focusing on keywords and see that there is an increase in the conversion rate, you can say you're getting high-quality traffic.

9.3 Tracking Keyword Rankings

After optimizing your website, it's crucial to monitor the performance of specific long-tail and targeted keywords. This can be achieved through a straightforward Google search for those specific keywords. Ideally, your goal is to secure the top position on the search engine results page (SERP), as approximately a quarter of users click on the first result.

Additionally, you can conduct a keyword gap analysis. This involves studying competing URLs and identifying the keywords that are driving their success. By understanding which keywords are effective for your competitors, you can refine and enhance your own list of keywords. This strategy can open doors to reaching previously untapped demographics.

Effective keyword ranking analysis allows you to stay competitive and adapt your SEO strategy to ensure your content remains visible and appealing to your target audience. Monitoring keyword rankings is an ongoing process that helps you maintain a strong online presence and drive organic traffic to your website.

9.4 Identification of Slow-Loading Pages

This aspect often goes unnoticed, but the time it takes for your web pages to load is a crucial indicator. If a page takes longer than 1-3 seconds to load, you are falling behind. Page loading speed is a significant factor in Google rankings, as mentioned earlier, and it is often assessed as a separate measure in evaluations due to its paramount importance.

A good analytics tool will provide metrics for various devices, allowing you to identify specific issues that need to be addressed individually. These data can then be communicated to programmers who can take action to optimize the pages.

9.5 Monitoring Engagement Metrics

There are many metrics that provide insights into user behavior. Here are some of the most popular ones.

Time on Page: Also known as "dwell time," this metric indicates how long visitors spend on a specific page. If they spend very little time on a long-form article, it's clear they are not reading it. However, if they only dedicate a few seconds to an "about me" page, the result might not be negative. Therefore, it's essential to consider time in relation to the type of content.

Pages per Visit: This metric indicates how many pages a visitor has viewed, offering insight into the level of engagement with the content. You can make content changes based on this metric or decide to leave it unchanged.

Bounce Rate: This metric represents the percentage of visitors who leave a page without further exploration. The bounce rate indicates whether visitors find the content quality engaging or not. However, it's important to note that this metric does not provide detailed information about the user experience. Sometimes, when a website is redesigned and improved, the bounce rate may increase before decreasing because users need to get used to the new layout. Therefore, it's crucial to carefully evaluate the data and rely on your judgment to interpret the results.

Chapter 10: Bringing It All Together

The realm of search engine optimization is vast and ever-evolving, with its depths filled with knowledge that could fill volumes. Congratulations on making it to the end of this journey. In this book, we've traversed the landscape of SEO, delving into the intricacies that make search engines appreciate and value your website.

From unraveling the essence of SEO to comprehending its universal significance across all types of websites, we've laid down the fundamental principles. You've embarked on a journey through the rich tapestry of terminology, gaining insights into the distinctions between virtuous practices and detrimental ones.

You've been made aware of the penalties that may befall those who disregard the rules, as well as the rewards that await those who play by them diligently. Along the way, we've explored the notion of shortcuts and why it's prudent to avoid them. We've also ventured into the realm of advanced SEO tactics, discovering that they can often be implemented with surprising simplicity.

It's worth noting that much of the SEO landscape can be entrusted to seasoned professionals armed with the knowledge and tools to navigate it swiftly and efficiently. However, if you find the time and resources to tackle this endeavor in-house, you free up valuable assets that can be channeled into the more creative aspects at the core of your operations.

Achieving that coveted high ranking on search engine results pages is akin to capturing the attention of a multitude of individuals, potentially transforming them into loyal customers for a lifetime. Such priceless engagement and loyalty are often beyond the reach of paid advertising alone.

As you conclude this journey, remember that SEO is not just a tool; it's a dynamic and strategic approach that, when mastered, can elevate your digital presence, enhance your credibility, and connect you with audiences far and wide. Keep honing your SEO skills, stay attuned to industry developments, and embrace the ever-changing landscape of digital marketing. Your continued commitment to SEO excellence will propel your online endeavors to new heights.

Thank you for joining us on this exploration of the fascinating world of SEO. We wish you all the success in your digital endeavors, and may your online presence shine brightly in the vast digital cosmos.

DigIdentity